D1607039

in
the
news™

BIOFUELS

SUSTAINABLE ENERGY IN THE 21ST CENTURY

Paula Johanson

ROSEN
PUBLISHING®

New York

For my father, who asked me why corn is used to make gasohol if sugarcane is many times more efficient

Published in 2010 by The Rosen Publishing Group, Inc.
29 East 21st Street, New York, NY 10010

First Edition

Library of Congress Cataloging-in-Publication Data

Johanson, Paula.
Biofuels: sustainable energy in the 21st century / Paula Johanson.—1st ed.
    p. cm.—(In the news)
Includes bibliographical references and index.
ISBN 978-1-4358-3584-9 (library binding)
ISBN 978-1-4358-8550-9 (pbk)
ISBN 978-1-4358-8551-6 (6 pack)
1. Biomass energy—Juvenile literature. I. Title.
TP339.J64 2010
333.95'39—dc22

2009021849

Manufactured in Malaysia

CPSIA Compliance Information: Batch #TWW10YA: For Further Information contact Rosen Publishing, New York, New York at 1-800-237-9932

On the cover: The owner of a diesel car *(top left)* can fill its fuel tank with high-quality biofuels from a number of sources, including fuels derived from tanks of algae *(top right)* or fields of corn *(bottom)*.

contents

A Progression of Fuels

Everywhere in the world, people use fuels to make fires for many purposes. There are fuels that are solids (wood and coal), fuels that are liquids (oil and alcohol), and others that are gases (natural gas). Some fuel is burned to cook food and do household tasks. Some is burned for industry, running machines that dig ores and smelt metal or do other useful tasks, such as spin thread and weave cloth on a scale larger than one person working at home. Some fuel is burned for transportation, consuming about a third of all the fuel that is used worldwide each year. There is a global need for fuels that are a sustainable energy source— fuels that can be renewed, that are reasonably easy to get and use, and that can be used without polluting the environment.

The first fuels that people used were biofuels—fuels derived from biological sources, as opposed to fossil fuels from geological sources. Usually, the sources of biofuels were plants, but there were animal sources as well. For thousands of years, people used wood as the primary biofuel. In places where there were few trees, people burned dried dung and bones instead, or twisted dried grasses into coils that would burn like sticks. People used vegetable oil in lamps. In the far north, people used animal fat as fuel for cooking.

The First Energy Crisis

Wood is easy to handle. But when it runs out, what will people use for fuel? "Seventeenth-century Britain was running out of wood," observes journalist Gwynne Dyer in his book *Climate Wars*. Coal was a natural option to try for a wood replacement. Coal had been a marginal fuel since ancient times.

Dyer and other commentators believe the British change to coal instead of wood kick-started the Industrial Revolution. Burning coal releases much more heat than the same amount of wood does. It became easier and cheaper to smelt iron and make steel using coal instead of wood for fuel. With affordable metals, machinery was made in greater quantities and varieties. In places like the Americas, where wood was still available, the economic benefits of the Industrial Revolution were delayed for another century.

"The turn of the twentieth century brought us into the fossil-fuel era. Sometime in the 1890s . . . we started getting more than half our energy from coal, oil, and gas, and as a result we started consuming radically more of it," says science journalist Robert Kunzig in *Discover* magazine. He and some energy experts have noted that as people get access to more ways of using energy, energy consumption per person increases. "One thing that humankind is not going to do in the twenty-first century as our population climbs . . . is consume less energy. In all likelihood, we are going to consume more." As human energy use increases, sustainable energy use becomes even more important.

Energy Source

The source of the energy that people use, perhaps to cook food or power a motor, is not the wood burning under the frying pan or the gasoline running into the engine. The wood and gasoline didn't create the energy; the energy came from sunlight falling on the earth and that energy was collected by plants and stored.

The sun's energy reaches the surface of the earth as sunlight. This solar energy warms the atmosphere and oceans, making warm air and water rise, creating currents. Humans can use these currents with windmills and turbines to run machinery. People can directly use solar energy, making buildings that are warmed passively by sunlight, and making solar collector panels of silicon that use sunlight to generate electricity. For many energy needs, solar energy is the most practical form of sustainable energy because the sun is not used up by human use of sunlight and there are many opportunities for the sustainable development of solar energy.

Plants also use solar energy. When plants grow and make food, they use the energy from sunlight to combine carbon dioxide (CO_2) and nitrogen (N) from the air, and water (H_2O) and other elements that they take up from the ground with their roots. Like all animals, humans need to eat food to fuel their bodies. People have also found that plants very effectively collect solar energy into substances like wood and oily seeds that are easy to handle, transport, store, and burn.

Solar energy is even the source of energy found in the fossil fuels coal, petroleum, and natural gas. "Fossil fuels are stored solar energy—sunlight that was captured millions or billions of years ago by animals, plants, algae, and bacteria," writes Kunzig, "buried and compressed into a useful form by the heat and weight of accumulating rock."

Besides energy, the material that made up the bodies of these plants, bacteria, algae, and animals is also stored in fuels. This organic material, with atoms of carbon, nitrogen, and hydrogen and other elements combined in molecules, has been stored in biofuels for days or years, and in fossil fuels as larger molecules for millions or billions of years. When people burn fuels, these atoms are returned to the atmosphere.

Up in Smoke

All fuels are not exactly alike. Although each fuel combines with oxygen from the air to create oxides and release heat, the products released by this reaction are not all the same. Some fuels release a great deal more heat when burned than the same amount of a different fuel will release. The kinds of smoke, soot, and gases released by various fuels didn't really matter to people for a long time. When the use of fuels increased during the Industrial Revolution, and again during the latter half of the twentieth century, people became aware of the polluting effects of burning various kinds of fuels.

The gases released by burning are called greenhouse gases because these gases allow sunlight to reach the earth's surface to warm the air and then trap the heat created by the sunlight. Some people think of these gases as being like a greenhouse that lets in light to warm the air inside the greenhouse and then traps the warm air inside the transparent roof and walls. When burned, biofuels release mostly CO_2 and a few other oxides, while fossil fuels additionally release other oxides as

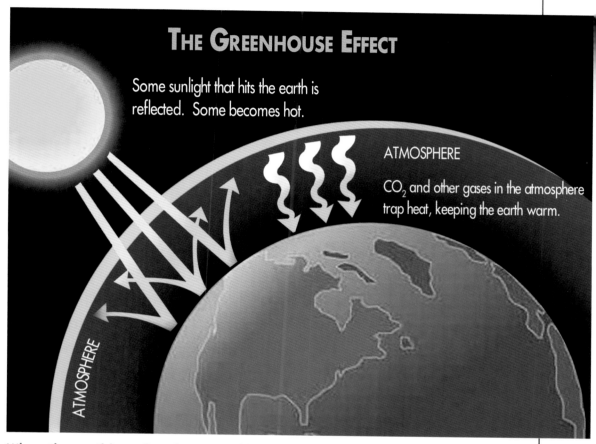

THE GREENHOUSE EFFECT

Some sunlight that hits the earth is reflected. Some becomes hot.

ATMOSPHERE

CO_2 and other gases in the atmosphere trap heat, keeping the earth warm.

ATMOSPHERE

When the earth's surface is warmed by sunlight, it radiates heat as infrared energy. Some of this energy escapes into space, but greenhouse gases trap more of the heat than oxygen and nitrogen in the atmosphere.

well as CO_2. The other gases released by burning fossil fuels are five or ten times as capable as CO_2 at the greenhouse gas effect, or even more.

When people burn biofuels, the CO_2 that left the air a few days or years ago to become part of the plant is returned to the atmosphere. When people burn fossil fuels, the gases released contain carbon that has been out of the atmosphere for millions or billions of years. The earth was a very different place when plants collected the gases that became the fossil fuels. When the most recent deposits were laid down, the world was warm enough that turtles and dinosaurs were living inside the Arctic Circle among swamps and forests, while most of the rest of the earth was desertlike. When the oldest deposits were laid down, tiny plants and animals that looked like flecked mats of mucky pond scum largely populated the world. These conditions were not good for modern plants, animals, and people.

As fossil fuels are burned, the return of long-stored gases to the atmosphere affects the earth's climate. There is now more CO_2 in the atmosphere than there has been for twenty million years. Burning biofuels also affects the climate, especially when large areas of vegetation are changed to grow the plants. If sustainable methods are used to grow, harvest, and burn biofuels, the effect on the climate can be much less than when fossil fuels are used. The goal is to have a fuel that is carbon-neutral, meaning that the fuel causes no net increase of carbon dioxide in the atmosphere.

Expectations for Energy Use

Humans are consuming greater amounts of energy each year. "One-fourth of all the oil consumed by humans in our entire history will be consumed from 2000 to 2010," Daniel Sperling and Deborah Gordon say in their book *Two Billion Cars*. "In the U.S., a transportation monoculture has taken root that's resistant to innovation. The rest of the world follows close behind." In industrialized nations, people have come to rely on transportation options. Many workers live farther than an hour's walk from the place where they work, so they depend on cars and buses to get to work. Most products made in factories are transported and sold to distant customers. Food is transported as well, not just from a farm to the nearest city, but across continents and around the world. The average North American dinner has traveled 1,500 to 3,000 miles (2,414 to 4,828 kilometers) from farm to plate. Fossil fuels are relied on for all of this transportation. There is a growing opportunity for sustainable energy use for transportation purposes, instead of fossil fuels.

"Greenhouse gas emissions continue to increase, even as scientific and political consensus has emerged that these emissions must be cut by 50 to 80 percent by 2050 if the climate is to be stabilized," report Sperling and Gordon. As they point out, "Until 2007, the United States was the largest emitter of greenhouse gases. Now, China is number one. Transportation is a big part of the problem. Globally, transportation produces about a fourth of all emissions of carbon dioxide [CO_2], the primary greenhouse gas." If the demand for transportation were reduced, this would reduce CO_2 emissions. Another way to reduce CO_2 emissions would be to replace fossil fuels with sustainable biofuels.

Modern or Old-Fashioned?

Biofuels are not old-fashioned fuels used only in the past or on camping trips. Even with the modern use of fossil fuels, hydroelectricity, and nuclear energy, writer John Twidell observes that approximately 10 percent of energy usage worldwide is still derived from biofuels. For example, millions of people throughout the world still cook their meals every day over simple open fires of burning wood or dried dung. There are advantages to using biofuels instead of fossil fuels for many purposes, from household use to industrial use to transportation purposes.

The disadvantages of various fuels must also be considered when making decisions about energy use. Hundreds of children in Africa are burned every year by falling into open cooking fires on the ground, for example. But fossil fuel stove alternatives are often far too expensive for families to afford. If small alcohol burners made from aluminum soft-drink cans were available and affordable for families, it might be easier to protect the

Many people cook over open fires. It is part of the Bedouin traditions enjoyed by this family celebrating the Muslim holy month of Ramadan in the Sinai desert of Egypt.

children. In addition, if alcohol biofuel were locally available and affordable, it would be a sustainable energy source. Families would not have to spend hours every day looking for wood to cook a meal. The United Nations' agencies working in the area of energy, through an interagency called UN-Energy, released a report in May 2007 saying that modern bioenergy holds "the promise of drastically reducing the death toll caused in developing countries by the 'kitchen killer'—

smoke inhalation, which is responsible for more fatalities each year than malaria."

Transportation Fuel

Most modern biofuels are being developed for transportation purposes, to replace gasoline or diesel fuel for use in internal combustion engines. It's worth noting that not all engines are like those in most cars and trucks, burning fuel inside a piston engine. The Lear Steam Car was a car powered by a working external combustion engine. Like the steam engine of a train, the engine of the Lear Steam Car was driven by steam. The source of the heat could be wood or coal. So few steam cars were ever built that they were never marketed as a profitable alternative to cars with internal combustion engines.

There are a few other special engines and vehicles that are being designed to make use of biofuels, but it's rare for these vehicles to be marketed to more than a few hundred customers. Instead, transportation alternatives are finding success and profit when biofuels are used in commonly available vehicles with ordinary engines.

"There are few problems technically; engines can generally cope with the new fuels," according to a biofuels report on the *BBC World News* Web site. "But current technologies limit production because only certain parts of specific plants can be used. The big hope is the so-called second generation of bio-fuels, which will process the cellulose found in many plants. This should lead to far more efficient production using a much greater range of plants and plant waste."

Biofuel labels at fuel pumps and on car bumpers are part of a growing trend in marketing cars and fuel. Biofuels can be used as conveniently as gasoline or diesel fuels.

"There is an urgent need to replace fossil oil, which returns long-stored carbon dioxide to the atmosphere when it is burned, with non-fossil fuels of similar properties, suitable for powering vehicles of every kind, that do not add to the long-term burden of carbon dioxide in the atmosphere," observes Gwynne Dyer. "Biofuels that absorb carbon dioxide as they grow, and release it again when they are burned, offer an attractive solution—*provided that* they do not displace food crops or forests, and that they really are carbon-neutral or close to it."

Existing Working Solutions from Biomass

"Biomass" is a term used to describe fuels that are produced by biological materials. These fuels can be liquids or gases, and they are energy sources comparable in many ways to fossil fuels. There are a couple of these biomass fuel alternatives that are already in use. They have the virtue of being compatible with existing technology. Instead of having to invent new engines for cars and trucks, there are biodiesel alternatives, such as vegetable oils, for existing diesel engines. In addition, biogas puts to good use the technology for pipes, tanks, and burners to handle propane and natural gas, with unique systems often being designed for particular applications.

Individual inventors can often design, construct, and use their own biomass systems as working solutions to their own energy needs. Energy experts anxious to not only make good use of fuel opportunities but also to manage this renewable resource wisely are promoting the wider application of biomass as biofuel for general public use.

This Brooklyn, New York, man mixes cooking oil from restaurants' deep fryers with diesel fuel to drive his truck and heat his home. He's one of many biofuel innovators, like author Greg Melville.

An Oily Solution

There is a biomass solution for transportation needs. The most practical supplement and replacement for existing uses for diesel fossil fuel is biodiesel—fuel from vegetable oil instead of petroleum. Fossil fuel isn't necessary to run an engine in a car or truck. When inventor Rudolf Diesel displayed his first diesel engine at the 1900 World's Fair, he ran it on peanut oil. It became common to use petroleum-based fuel when the price for fossil fuel dropped below that of vegetable oil.

A diesel fuel engine will start up best with diesel when the engine is cold. But once the engine is running and warm, the fuel can have vegetable oil added. The motor will even run on pure canola oil. The 2009 and newer models of catalytic converter must be placed so that the exhaust gases are very hot or else the converter will lower fuel efficiency as it reduces emissions.

In North America, biodiesel is usually made from canola seed (also known by its older name, rapeseed), but it can be made from corn oil or soybeans. It's not necessary to use new oil; biodiesel can be made from oil that has been used in restaurant deep fryers. In tropical countries, biodiesel is made from palm oil.

Putting Greenhouse Gas to Good Use

Methane is a gas that is naturally produced by the decay of organic materials. Many garbage dumps and landfills have methane seeping up through layers of buried garbage. Agricultural sites are producers of methane, from rotting plant materials and manure. Sewage treatment lagoons bubble with rising methane. Nearly all of this gas is allowed to blow away on the wind as a troublesome stink, which is explosive if it collects, and has been known to smother farm workers. "Methane is particularly problematic because it is about twenty times as potent per molecule as a greenhouse gas as carbon dioxide is," says John P. Holdren, an energy and environment expert (and a science adviser for President Barack Obama's cabinet), as quoted in *Climate Wars*.

Rather than allow methane to leak into the atmosphere, people can collect this gas when possible, as a fuel called biogas. It is not difficult to capture the methane as it leaks from a landfill, a manure containment structure, or a sewage treatment lagoon. The landfill's garbage is unchanged, and the manure is still good to use for compost. The cost of a methane capture system is soon made up by the energy released by burning the biogas. Some biogas systems are used to heat buildings. Others generate electricity or fuel vehicles. Each system is often a custom modification of pipes, tanks, and burners originally invented for use with propane gas or natural gas.

As a greenhouse gas, methane is alarmingly effective. "This methane is twenty-two times worse than carbon dioxide [as a warming agent]," states NASA scientist Dennis Mueller in *Climate Wars*. There is a net reduction in greenhouse gases produced by a landfill or manure when methane is burned as biogas instead of being wasted.

It's odd to think of a landfill as a service provider with a carbon footprint, like a restaurant that has fresh seafood flown in every week. Most farmers and agricultural corporations never consider that cattle in a feedlot generate enough biogas to meet the transportation needs for the feedlot's trucks. Some people are

The National Renewable Energy Laboratory wants to further commercially develop biofuel, solar, and wind technologies.

offended by the idea of using biogas from garbage dumps or sewage treatment plants, while others believe it is more offensive to waste the naturally occurring bio-gas. Changes in human expectations are needed to bring biofuels from the marginal alternatives realm into the mainstream of sustainable energy usage worldwide.

Defining Agrofuel

Not all biofuels are alike. Some are better defined as agrofuels rather than sustainable fuels that make use of available energy opportunities. "Agrofuels are biofuels made from crops and trees grown specifically for that purpose on a large scale, as well as biofuels from agricultural and forest residues that should be returned to the natural cycle because they play an important role in maintaining soil fertility and biodiversity," writes a representative for the Sustainable Biodiesel Alliance, a nonprofit society promoting the sustainable biodiesel industry. "Biofuels from true waste, such as biogas from manure or landfill, or waste vegetable oil, are not agrofuels. Biofuels from algae are not agrofuels either." By this reasoning, growing soybeans or palm oil for biodiesel would make that fuel an agrofuel, a product of agriculture.

Solution or New Problem?

There's an old saying: if you're not part of the solution, you're part of the problem. Unfortunately, biofuels can be part of the solution for energy usage, but at the same time part of the problem of unsustainable development. "Biofuels work," says Dr. Frank Zeeman, director of the Center for Metropolitan Sustainability at the New York Institute of Technology. "But they have a big environmental impact." Biodiesel can be produced in ways that have adverse environmental and economic effects.

Sustainable development means that a product is not made just for the money that can be earned by selling it. A sustainably developed project will support the biodiversity of a region instead of replacing, for example, the many plant species of a tallgrass prairie with a single species of canola patented by a large agricultural company. "Lucrative palm oil prices inspire the destruction of environmentally priceless rainforests to make way for palm plantations," reports staff writer Anduin Kirkbride McElroy for *Biodiesel Magazine*. The oil-rich seeds of palm trees can produce up to 650 gallons (2,460 liters) of oil per acre. When soybeans need good farming land to produce a mere 50 or so gallons (about 220 l) of oil per acre, entrepreneurs might see palm trees as a valuable alternative to rainforests. It's hard to put a dollar value on undiscovered medicinal plants or an ecosystem large enough to support many plant and animal species. But palm seeds sell for cash.

McElroy goes on to quote a prediction from the independent research organization Worldwatch Institute that "a surge in jatropha plantings for biodiesel production 'will likely pull the last string of ecological collapse' in environmentally sensitive southwestern China, where natural forests are already shrinking rapidly." If biodiesel is produced from plants grown in ways that do not support the economic development of a community, there can be disastrous results for people who depend on the traditional diverse ecology and those who have pinned all of their hopes on the shaky chances for success of a single monoculture crop.

Biomass Can Be Green

Many energy experts promote the use of biomass as a possible "zero net CO_2" energy source, which would not contribute to increased greenhouse gas production. "The zero net CO_2 argument relies on the assumption

Government programs need citizens to participate, like these students in the Philippines. They are planting more than five hundred thousand trees along the Pan-Philippine Highway to reduce pollution.

that new trees, or other crops, will be replanted to the extent that they will absorb any CO_2 released during the consumption of biomass energy," observes writer Robert Evans. "This may well be true for properly managed 'energy plantations,' but is not likely to pertain in many developing countries where most of the biomass energy is obtained from forests which are not being replanted, at least to the same degree that they are being harvested." Biomass plantings and harvesting will be managed responsibly only with attention from national and international authorities, and the enforcement of industry guidelines at high-but-achievable levels for business practices.

Ethanol and Ethics

For thousands of years, people have been using yeast to make alcohol and carbon dioxide—alcohol in wine or beer, and bubbles of CO_2 to leaven bread. Yeast, when dry, looks like little grains of millet or tiny balls of clay, but it is actually a living animal. Inside those little balls are tiny one-celled organisms, too small to see, that when mixed with water are released and become active. If there is sugar or starch in the mix, the tiny yeast cells will eat the sugar or starch, and release both alcohol and carbon dioxide gas as their wastes. This process is called fermentation. It is essential in the production of ethyl alcohol, a common biofuel also called ethanol.

The process of making alcohol fuel from plants is more like making wine or beer than it is like baking bread. When fruit juice or mashed grain is mixed with water and a bit of yeast, the sugars or starches in the liquid are changed to alcohol, making wine or beer. The carbon dioxide gas bubbles up out of the liquid, while the alcohol remains in the liquid.

Ethanol makes a good fuel for a lamp, a small burner of a campstove, or an internal combustion engine. "Thirty percent of this year's U.S. grain harvest will go straight to ethanol distilleries," wrote Gwynne Dyer in *Climate Wars* in 2008. Ethanol biofuel can be processed in small factories close to where the plant materials are grown and close to where it will be used. Newt Gingrich, former speaker of the House of Representatives and coauthor of *A Contract with the Earth*, believes that biofuel "holds promise as a domestic alternative to oil acquired from totalitarian regimes."

Changes in Demand

Until 2008, it was easy to believe that ethanol would be the transportation fuel of the future. "Congress had mandated the doubling of corn ethanol use, to 15 billion gallons [more than 56 billion liters] by 2015," reports Clifford Krauss for the *New York Times*. Because the soaring cost per barrel of oil was raising gasoline prices, refiners were willing to try to keep the cost at the pump a little more affordable by blending in ethanol, which is cheaper than gasoline. But the recession beginning in late 2008 brought down the price per barrel of crude oil, as well as customers' demand for gasoline.

As Krauss phrased it, "Refiners [had] little incentive to use more ethanol than they are required to use."

The ethanol industry invests in production equipment, such as these stainless-steel fermentation tanks in Gibson City, Illinois. Changes in the economy and in energy prices affect usage and profits.

Declining customer consumption of gasoline with only 10 percent ethanol added means less market pressure "for the development of more advanced biofuels, like ethanol made from switchgrass and wood chips . . . The ethanol industry is now pressing the Obama administration to raise the 10 percent blend limit in most gasoline blends to as high as 15 percent to bolster demand for biofuels."

A higher percentage of ethanol blended into gasoline does not cause problems for most vehicles that are used for personal transportation. "The argument that ethanol is inferior to diesel and gasoline is not valid," writes James Nash, a climate scientist for the nonprofit environmental organization Greatest Planet, pointing out that pure ethanol has many advantages as a fuel. "Most importantly, it mixes with water. With advanced engine technology, it can outperform gasoline 2 to 1, or better."

Ethanol for Energy Independence

Americans' use of ethanol as a transportation fuel blended into gasoline began during Richard M. Nixon's presidency (1969–1974). Ethanol wasn't seen then as an environmentally green fuel but more as a way of using up excess corn produced by agricultural corporations that were subsidized by the federal government. "When the United States [began] to subsidize the conversion of corn into ethanol . . . the stated purpose was, in President George W. Bush's phrase, 'energy independence,'" Dyer writes in *Climate Wars*. He points out that the intent was to replace imported oil, "which was subject to sudden price fluctuations and to politically motivated interruptions of supply, with a home-grown source of fuel that was always available and not too expensive. At the time, nobody even calculated whether it was carbon-neutral or not."

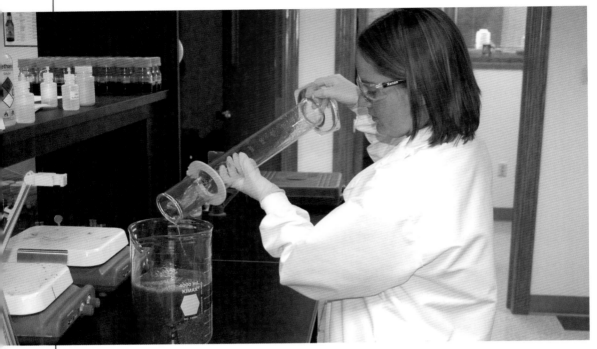

A fermentation research analyst works in a lab in Sioux Falls, South Dakota, for a corn-based ethanol production company. The company is researching ways to produce ethanol from cellulose.

"People think it [ethanol]'s a very green fuel," comments Michael Pollan, author of *In Defense of Food*, "but the process for making it is not green at all." Evans quotes a study in *Fueling Our Future* that found "the production of ethanol required between 29 percent and 57 percent more fossil energy than is produced in the form of ethanol, depending upon the [plant] source chosen."

When the crops for biofuel are being grown on existing farmland, there are large energy inputs involved in planting, tending, and harvesting the crop, and converting it into biofuel, which "often means that there are large net emissions of greenhouse gases," writes Dyer. "But when forest is being cleared to grow biofuels . . . the equations involved become quite insane." Dyer quotes a recent study in the U.S. journal *Science*, calculating that destroying natural ecosystems to grow crops for biofuels releases CO_2, between 17 and 420 times more than will be saved annually by burning the biofuel grown on that land instead of fossil fuel. "It's all justified in the name of fighting climate change, but the numbers just don't add up," says Dyer.

Aquifer Use

In 2009, as Jane Braxton Little reports for *Scientific American*, "biofuels are the latest enticement to grow corn, which garners higher profits but requires more water than most other crops." When there is insufficient surface water to grow crops, as in the U.S. heartlands, water is pumped up from deep underground to irrigate fields. The Ogallala aquifer is an underground water resource that would take six thousand years to refill once drained. "Plans to double the number of ethanol production facilities in the High Plains region are driving farmers to increase corn production despite already scarce groundwater," Little notes. The Environmental Defense Fund warns that an additional 120 billion gallons (more than 454 billion liters) of Ogallala could be pumped up annually to meet this increased irrigation. While the United States is seeking energy independence, pumping an irreplaceable water resource dry to make ethanol would not be sustainable energy development.

Ethanol Ethics

There are other values to consider in addition to the worth of transportation fuel. "Many are under the mistaken idea that ethanol comes only from rice and corn," observes journalist Stephanie Berthiaume on a technology Web site. "As a result, the prices of grains have skyrocketed for fear of a food shortage, making life even harder for millions who are struggling to get by on a day-to-day basis. Charging more for foodstuffs under the premise that they should be or are being used to power cars rather than feed the hungry is unethical— but it is not necessary."

On an energy information Web site, journalist Sharon Astyk reduces the impact of biofuels on world hunger to simple land use mathematics. "For example, were we to convert all 179,000 hectares [about 442,318 acres] of arable land in the U.S. to biofuel production, we might be able to meet much of our present energy needs," Astyk notes. Unfortunately, there would be no farmland to grow food.

Microbes Contributing to Big Solutions

Existing ways of converting plant materials into biofuels use seeds and starches or sugars instead of the entire plant. New methods of creating biofuels are being tested and brought into production, offering opportunities to use the cellulose commonly found in most plants. Unfortunately, each method has effects on the environment and the communities of people using the marginally fertile lands that would be needed to grow biofuel crops. More than one solution is needed for biofuels to solve the sustainable energy question.

New Generation Fuels

"Once seen as a promising alternative to gasoline, corn-based ethanol is being supplanted by a second generation of biofuels promising greater sustainability," according to Simon Robinson, a spokesman for ICIS Chemical Business, a marketing information service for

Fermentation tanks at the National Renewable Energy Laboratory require operators and researchers to develop ways for industries to profit, making ethanol from cellulose in plants.

the petrochemical and energy industry. "Cellulosic materials, algae, pyrolysis, and directed evolution are all contributing to these developments," says Robinson. Each of these options for future fuels is worth discussion on its own. Algae grow without crowding out land-based plants. Pyrolysis is a heat treatment that owes much to the pulp and paper industry. Robinson is using directed evolution as a euphemism for genetically modified organisms. The use of cellulosic materials is just emerging as a biofuel opportunity.

"The second-generation or 'cellulosic' biofuels, made from switch-grass, willow, or other fast-growing plants raised on land marginal for agriculture, hold considerable promise for the mid-term future," writes Dyer in *Climate Wars*. These biofuels use plant materials with a high cellulose content. A heat treatment at 500 degrees Fahrenheit (260 degrees Celsius) called pyrolysis (controlled combustion without bursting into flame) converts the biomass of plant materials like straw into a slurry. The slurry contains around 90 percent of the bio-energy of the straw and is easily stored in tanks and silos or transported for further refine-ment. When reheated with steam, the slurry produces syn-thesis gas, which can be used as biofuel.

Pyrolysis of jatropha (oilseed) and bamboo and other plants with plenty of cellulose can be done, producing bio-char (which can be used as a soil conditioner, but its effectiveness for long-term carbon storage is not proven), bio-oil, and synthesis gas. The latter two can be used for heat and power generation, or as precursors to transportation fuel.

In the long run, biofuels from plants like algae or halophyte (salt-tolerant) plants that can be grown in stagnant or salty water may be even better. Dyer goes

Oil seeds

Typical oil extraction by selected seed (oil content per seed):

Sesame	**50%**
Jatropha	**37%**
Rapeseed	**37%**
Oil palm kernel	**36%**
Mustard	**35%**
Sunflower	**32%**
Oil palm fruit	**20%**
Soybean	**14%**
Cotton seed	**13%**

Jatropha seeds are considered one of the best sources for future biodiesel production

Biofuel makers care about the oil content of seeds and the work to grow and harvest the plants. While cotton needs to be farmed, oil palms grow with much less work.

on to call the current generation of biofuels grown on croplands an almost unmitigated disaster. He believes that if the subsidies are not cut back and the farmland restored to food production, there almost certainly will be an absolute shortage of food in the world in only a very few years. "In that case, the poor will be starving so that the rich can drive their automobiles on what they imagine is a more eco-friendly fuel. One cannot imagine a political environment less conducive to global concentration on climate-change issues."

How Marginal Is Marginal?

Growing plants for ethanol on marginal land is not an automatic solution. The crop will crowd out the natural ecosystem in areas that may not be sustained by the planting and harvesting processes. Marginal land is exactly that: it is marginal farmland for any of a multitude of reasons. The soil may be marginally fertile. The terrain may be subject to erosion. The land may be barely manageable for agriculture because of elevation, drainage, or other factors that will make it marginal for the purpose of growing crops for ethanol, even tough locally appropriate plants like yellow willow along riverbanks in Montana. And because the land is marginal, people who are not settled farmers may rely it on for nomadic use. Marginal lands may also be ecologically

Traditional methods for planting rice in flooded fields near Vientiane, Laos, make specialized use of land. Croplands and marginal lands are vulnerable to being taken over for agrofuels.

sensitive territory supporting unique biodiversity in plants and animals.

"Marginal lands support a multitude of livelihoods but also have a critical ecological role," observes Helena Paul in an article on biofuels. "Such lands can be vital for local people, yet they may be invisible to policymakers, conveniently so for corporate agendas." She raises the point that in many developing nations, such as Laos and Namibia, women's agricultural work does not take place on fenced, fertile fields. "Agrofuels production might cause the partial or total displacement of women's agricultural activities," says Paul.

Genetically Modified Yeast

There is research being done to make genetically modified versions of yeast. These genetically modified organisms (GMOs) would turn cellulose, as well as sugars and starches, into alcohol fuels. These GMO yeasts would be no good for making bread or beer, but they would be useful for making fuels from plant materials that currently have no agricultural use.

Frankenfood or Frankenfuel?

GMO yeast is a frightening concept for some researchers. The new forms of yeast being invented are patented and owned by the designers. But there is a lot more to think about than what to name the invention. Yeast lives in the wild, blowing on the wind, living in animals, and lying dormant in the dust till it finds moisture and carbohydrates.

What if GMO yeast escapes from a lab or factory? Yeast can be carried out of a secure laboratory accidentally, inside the body of a researcher. It's fair to ask if GMO yeast will be similarly able to live inside human and animal bodies, and if it will have effects that are similar to wild yeast.

What happens if GMO yeast crosses with wild yeasts? Although single-cell organisms reproduce on their own without mating, they also share genes with each other. Any modified genes would be carefully chosen and placed in the GMO yeast's DNA. But the genetic dice would be rolled if GMO yeast ever did share its genes with a wild yeast. The resulting crossbreed might use the modified genes in unintended ways that could have bad effects on people or animals.

Algae

Algae grow like pond scum, without any of the plowing, fertilizing, and weeding of field crops, such as corn and sugar cane. Algae are a natural choice for a biological source of fuel. They are already 40 percent oil, just as they grow naturally. In addition, many kinds of alga do not need fresh water but can grow in brackish water in lagoons or in salt water.

Biodiesel made from algae is the best candidate for a biofuel that will work in the jet engines of airplanes. "In fact," David Biello, who writes on energy and the environment, reports in an article in *Scientific American*, "the alternative jet fuel . . . has as good or better qualities

This algae farming pond in eastern Virginia brings the owner an income selling algae to a nearby university, where it is made into biodiesel fuel. Making biodiesel fuel from algae is an emerging business opportunity.

than [petroleum-based fuel]: it does not freeze at high-altitude temperatures, delivers the same or more power to the engines, and is lighter as well."

Another issue that must be considered when discussing algae use is the current conditions for algae growing naturally in the oceans. The oceans' capacity to absorb carbon dioxide out of the atmosphere provides a natural "carbon sink." This absorption is called a sink because just as water going down a drain is no longer a problem in a kitchen, the CO_2 absorbed would no longer be a greenhouse gas raising the temperature of the earth's atmosphere.

"[A]bout half of the [world's] carbon dioxide sink is in the oceans. This is the absorption of carbon dioxide by the water and its utilization by the algae," explains NASA executive Dennis Mueller in *Climate Wars*. Though much of the algae in the oceans grows offshore, out of sight, it is affected by what humans do on land. Mueller points out that because people now have planted winter wheat and changed the land cover, vast amounts of iron-rich dust no longer drift out over the ocean, and algae require iron-rich dust. "So 30 to 40 percent of the algae [have] gone over the last several decades, say the NASA officials. And because of the carbon dioxide absorption into the water, the water is turning into carbonic acid, which is further killing the algae." Mueller estimates from recent measurements that about half of the carbon dioxide uptake in the oceans is gone. Algae farming for biofuel production may become a valuable opportunity for taking CO_2 out of the atmosphere, even if only temporarily.

5 The Best Biofuel

There is a gap between theory and practice when it comes to global responsible use of biofuels for sustainable energy. Theories alone aren't much use without practical development of business methods and products designed to meet energy needs both effectively and efficiently. Moreover, even the best products and tools are of no use when hungry people are not supported by a stable environment and government. The world's leading energy thinkers are applying their ingenuity to finding practical biofuel solutions to real problems in energy use. The use of biofuels is believed by scientists like David Suzuki and analysts like Ken Wiwa to be an essential part of future energy use, which must be sustainable if climate catastrophe and global conflicts are to be avoided.

Now that it's becoming increasingly obvious that people need to make good choices about using biofuels, one of the questions that some people ask is, "Which is the best biofuel?" There are several answers to this question, depending on who is asking, where they are, and what they are doing with the fuel. There is also one answer that is right for everyone.

The Human Contribution

The best biofuel is the effort a person puts into the application of energy to a project. This effort can be moving objects with our bodies' strength. It can also be thinking about what work is to be done. People can consciously choose the best mechanical approach to a project, the best use of transport, and the best fuel for each purpose. The most renewable resource in the world is the human effort to do things well: to work, create, and be considerate of yourselves, one another, and the world.

Even if the best biofuel is human effort, it still needs to be applied wisely. The answer is not merely, "I will work harder," as the draft horse Boxer responded to every new challenge in George Orwell's *Animal Farm*. Overwork and exhaustion are not solutions to energy needs, as Orwell makes clear in his novel, particularly not when the worker is treated like a resource that can be used up for other people's benefit, without consideration or even compensation.

Human effort is already being applied as a partial solution to fuel needs. BBC journalist Richard Bilton

These Brazilian men and women harvest sugarcane from the burned fields of a plantation. Laws protect worker safety but are not enforced in the hills far from cities where cane is processed into ethanol.

observes that the cheap cost of human work in Brazil is one reason why sugarcane is such a cost-efficient source of ethanol compared with corn. Bilton suggests that if the half-million Brazilian men working as *cutaderos* harvesting sugarcane were paid the low wages of North American farm workers, the cane would cost five to ten times as much to harvest. This increased cost of production would affect the price paid by customers buying fuel.

Human effort is also being overapplied toward the primary fossil fuel being used in China: coal. Sharon LaFraniere reports for the *New York Times* on how coal is made available in China because of underpaid workers who put in long hours in dangerous mines that don't meet safety standards common in Western countries. Russian coal miners are dedicated workers, too, and have continued to mine coal even when they have not been paid for months. These workers understand that there are few alternatives to making fuel available in the middle of winter in northern latitudes. Energy analyst Helen Paul believes that this work ethic has set a precedent that may end up being applied when workers are trying to make scrubby fields of jatropha survive in China for agrofuel or harvest wild grasses in Siberia for biogas. As Paul observes in *Ecologist* magazine, safety standards and fair pay are human rights that are often sacrificed when workers are cold and hungry and hard work is their only opportunity.

Legislating the Intentional Change to Biofuels

Global usage of biofuels is affected by the legislation passed in each country establishing intended energy use for the future. In the Energy Independence and Security Act of 2007, the U.S. Congress set a target of using 36 billion gallons (212 billion liters) of biofuels per year by the year 2022, of which only 15 billion gallons (56.8 billion liters) can be corn ethanol. Twenty-one billion

The economic stimulus bill signed by President Barack Obama recognizes that renewable energy technology is an important part of the economy of a nation—and the world.

gallons (79.5 billion liters) must be advanced biofuels: 16 billion gallons (60.5 billion liters) of cellulosic ethanol and 5 billion gallons (almost 19 billion liters) of biodiesel. Clifford Krauss reports for the *New York Times* that this is "a goal some energy experts say will be difficult to reach unless the economy grows robustly over the next several years."

The U.S. economic recovery bill that President Obama signed into law on February 17, 2009, included an investment of more than $76 billion into renewable energy and technology for energy efficiency. This amount sets a good example for Western nations. For instance, it was more than six times greater on a per capita basis than a similar announcement made in Canada's federal budget two months earlier. The British government passed a similar law, requiring that by 2010, 5 percent of the fuel sold at the pump in Britain had to be a biofuel.

Carbon tax is another form of legislation intended to promote the use of non-combustion energy sources—solar, wind, hydroelectricity, and nuclear power—as well as sustainable biofuels by discouraging the use of fossil fuels. This is an environmental tax on emissions of greenhouse gases like carbon dioxide. Because the tax is in proportion to the carbon content of a fuel and is levied at the sale of a product, it is a highly visible tax and is effective at reducing consumption.

The International Industrial Revolution

"The 'energy problem,' that is, the provision of a sustainable and non-polluting energy supply to meet all of our domestic, commercial, and industrial energy needs, is a complex and long-term challenge for society," observes writer Robert Evans, professor of clean energy systems at the University of British Columbia, Vancouver. This challenge is being faced by an increasing number of nations around the world. As developing nations increase their industrialization, there is understandable opposition to any advice from the United States or United Nations to restrict the developing nations' increasing energy use.

"When the U.S. tries to tell China to reduce its carbon emissions, the people there have a pretty effective response," author Greg Melville points out. He says the argument is hard to answer. "They usually say something like, 'You heedlessly polluted the air for more than a century, starting with the Industrial Revolution," Melville notes. "Why are you trying to hinder our industrial revolution?'"

The approach taken by Hillary Rodham Clinton, the U.S. secretary of state, on a 2009 visit to China took a new tack, paraphrased by Melville in excerpts from his book, *Greasy Rider*. "'You have a right to improve your standard of living, but we'd like you to follow greener practices so you don't make the same mistakes [regarding the environment] that we've made.' It's a surprisingly humble approach." This approach avoids the impression of colonialism by imperialist Western nations. It gets better results than trying to impose international standards without discussion.

International Meetings

National leaders have made it their business to represent their countries at international gatherings on the impact of biofuels on national economies. Biofuels were an important element of the agendas of the G20 Summit in London, England, and the Fifth Summit of the Americas in Port of Spain, Trinidad, both held in April 2009. "Washington is pushing for increased government spending," analyst Jeff Mason reports for Reuters News, "while countries such as France favor more emphasis on tough market regulation." Unfortunately, the world's leaders don't all speak with one voice. "Separately, Mr. Obama acknowledged that U.S. tariffs on Brazilian shipments of ethanol to the United States had been 'a source of tension' that would not change overnight." Mason further explains that Brazilian ethanol producers were upset during the G20 Summit that the United States still levied "a 54-cent import tariff on each gallon of exported Brazilian ethanol. American ethanol producers, who receive government subsidies, are worried ethanol imports would flood the U.S. market and hurt their business."

Unequal Access to Energy Use

People around the world don't all make the same use of fuels at work and at home. "Although the United States makes up only 5 percent of the world's population, we consume 28 percent of the world's energy," says Newt Gingrich in his book *A Contract with the Earth*. He adds that "at current usage, 78 percent of our energy consumption is from fossil fuels." Like many people writing on energy usage, Gingrich believes that many uses for fossil fuels can be met with biofuels, particularly ones that are sustainably made.

Other commentators draw attention to the unequal benefits from current fuel usage. While millions of people cook their families' meals over an open fire, fueled in India by gathering dried cow dung or in Africa by walking for an hour or two each day to collect a few sticks, the populations of industrialized nations have access to appliances in kitchens that use more energy than a third world health clinic. "It is essential that the biofuels industry be developed in ways that spread the economic benefits as widely as possible," says Suzanne Hunt, biofuels expert for Worldwatch Institute, in *Biofuels Magazine*, "rather than replicating the disastrous concentration of wealth that has marked the petroleum industry in countries such as Nigeria and Saudi Arabia."

The UN Takes a Stand

The United Nations energy division, UN-Energy, released a report in May 2007 providing a framework for sustainable methods of bioenergy use. "Unless new policies are enacted to protect threatened lands, secure socially acceptable land use, and steer bioenergy development in a sustainable direction overall," the report warns, "the environmental and social damage could in some cases outweigh the benefits." The report advises that national decision makers consider the social costs and economic intents of subsidizing liquid biofuels, and create policies that take into account availability, access, stability, and utilization of bioenergy alternatives.

The UN-Energy Web site (http://esa.un.org/un-energy) is only one of many online sources for government and corporate information about biofuels and renewable energy technology.

Local Government Participation

Every level of government has a role to play in energy usage decisions. "Municipalities throughout the nation continue to take small but important steps," observes Gingrich. "Portland [Oregon]'s greenhouse gas emissions have receded to 1990 levels, compared with national increases of some 16 percent. By all accounts, the measures taken by local industry and government have actually improved the economy. City fathers advocated conversion from diesel to biodiesel, and they have legislated a 10 percent ethanol requirement for other vehicles." Instead of waiting for federal programs, municipal and state governments can exercise their local authority and exceed federal standards.

"The danger with biofuels is that extremely valuable forests will be destroyed unnecessarily," says former U.S. vice president Al Gore, who was awarded the Nobel Peace Prize for his efforts to promote worldwide awareness of climate change. In 2008, Gore called for sustainable biofuels and "a CO_2 tax that is then rebated back to the people progressively, according to the laws of each nation in ways that shift the burden of taxation from employment to pollution."

More Than Three R's

Recycling programs and media promotion have made the Three R's of recycling into a household slogan: Reduce, Reuse, Recycle! But there are other R's that apply to the process of making biofuel choices:

- Rethink the purpose for which fuel is being used.
- Refuse to accept wasteful products and packaging.
- Repurpose existing fuel products and resources for new goals.
- Redesign ineffective and inefficient products and methods.

- Reject unsustainable methods.
- Reconsider the consequences of goals and choices.

Barbara Ehrenreich writes in *This Land Is Their Land* that the wealthy in Western nations use energy consumption as "a sign of status" for luxuries like setting air-conditioning down to 68°F (20°C) in the summer. "You burn up all the BTUs you can. Expect joules to start replacing jewels as a key marker of wealth." Ehrenrich suggests that wiser signs of status to admire are modest energy consumption and responsible energy use, such as the 2009 fad of hosting "100-Mile Dinners" in which serving food that had not been transported thousands of miles was the intent.

"Whether or not fossil fuel–hungry humans can admit it right now," says Kunzig when profiling energy alternatives, "from a distance the fossil fuel era will be just a blip in human history." Sustainable biofuels are not only the fuels of the future; they are also essential products for immediate development. Necessary for maintaining the environment and avoiding international conflict, biofuels are a fascinating opportunity for personal energy use and sustainable business practices worldwide.

Glossary

agrofuel Fuel made from an agricultural product, such as grain, plant products, or wood waste from logging.

biofuel Fuel, such as wood, oil, or alcohol; it is derived from biological sources, as opposed to fossil fuels that are derived from geological sources.

biomass Organic plant and animal material, especially waste matter, which is used as a source of fuel.

carbon dioxide sink The absorption of carbon dioxide into a substance, effectively removing CO_2 from the atmosphere; the largest available CO_2 sink is the ocean.

carbon neutral A process that compensates for releasing CO_2 into the atmosphere by the creation of new CO_2 sinks, often by planting trees for reforestation.

carbon tax A tax levied by a government on the purchase of goods or services, using a sliding scale based on the amount of CO_2 released into the atmosphere during the manufacturing or delivery, intended to discourage production of CO_2.

crossbreed An animal or plant produced by mating or hybridizing two different species, breeds, or varieties.

ethanol Ethyl alcohol; an organic molecule produced as a waste product of yeast.

fossil fuel Fuel, such as petroleum, coal, or natural gas, which is derived from a geological source.

joule A unit of energy, convenient for measuring production of heat in furnaces; the metric joule can be compared to watts or to British thermal units (BTUs).

GMO A genetically modified organism; GMOs have had their DNA altered in laboratories, usually with additions from similar organisms, though DNA from fish or animals is sometimes added to plant DNA.

green A product or service described as "green" makes environmentally responsible use of resources, particularly nonrenewable ones; there is no national or industry standard for green products or services.

greenhouse gas A gas that is transparent in sunlight but traps heat radiating up from the earth's surface, functioning like a glass roof in a greenhouse; carbon dioxide (CO_2) is the most common greenhouse gas.

monoculture Agriculture that grows a single type of plant in large areas, such as a field of canola patented by a large corporation instead of a mixed boreal forest of bushes and deciduous and conifer trees.

oxide A compound of an element or a substance that combines with oxygen.

per capita For each person in a population.

pyrolysis A heat treatment of controlled combustion, converting plant materials into bio-char that can be composted, and bio-oil and synthesis gas that can be converted into transportation fuels.

For More Information

Abundance Foundation

Box 1113

Pittsboro, NC 27312

(919) 533-5181

Web site: http://theabundancefoundation.org

The Abundance Foundation educates people and increases public awareness of sustainable energy usage. The foundation supports projects developing renewable energy ideas, local food systems, and community-aware businesses.

Center for Ecoliteracy

2528 San Pablo Avenue

Berkeley, CA 94702

(510) 845-4595

Web site: http://www.ecoliteracy.org

The Center for Ecoliteracy offers practical resources for parents, educators, and students interested in education for sustainable living. Its community-based approach includes using seminars, teaching guides, books, and consulting.

David Suzuki Foundation

Suite 219, 2211 West Fourth Avenue

Vancouver, BC V6K 4S2

Canada

(800) 453-1533

Web site: http://www.davidsuzuki.org

The David Suzuki Foundation uses science and education to promote solutions that conserve nature and help achieve sustainability within a generation. Focusing on four program areas, including climate change and clean energy, the foundation works to find ways for society to live in balance with the natural world that sustains us.

National Biodiesel Board

P.O. Box 104898

Jefferson City, MO 65110-4898

(573) 635-3893

Web site: http:// www.biodiesel.org

The National Biodiesel Board is the national trade association representing the biodiesel industry in the United States. Founded in 1992 by state soybean commodity groups, it has developed into an industry association of processor organizations, suppliers, marketers and distributors, and technology providers. The mission of the board is to create sustainable biodiesel industry growth.

Pembina Institute

200, 608 – Seventh Street SW

Calgary, AB T2P 1Z2

Canada

(403) 269-3344

Web site: http://www.pembina.org

The Pembina Institute works to advance sustainable energy solutions through research, education, consulting, and advocacy.

The institute maintains offices in Ottawa and Toronto, as well as Calgary, Edmonton, Vancouver, Yellowknife, and Drayton Valley. There are directors to answer inquiries on such issues as renewable energy, sustainable communities, green learning, and more.

Transportation Sustainability Research Center
University of California Berkeley
Richmond Field Station
1301 South 46th Street, Building 190
Richmond, CA 94804-4648
(510) 665-3451
Web site: http://www.its.berkeley.edu/sustainabilitycenter
The Transportation Sustainability Research Center conducts research on alternate transportation fuels, advanced vehicle technologies, transportation and environmental policy, and innovative mobility strategies. The center engages in outreach to improve understanding of the economic, environmental, and social aspects of transportation systems, and to actively participate in developing energy systems that support a sustainable world.

Web Sites

Due to the changing nature of Internet links, Rosen Publishing has developed an online list of Web sites related to the subject of this book. This site is updated regularly. Please use this link to access this list:

http://www.rosenlinks.com/itn/biof

For Further Reading

Ashton, Tim, and We Are What We Do. *Change the World for Ten Bucks: 50 Actions to Change the World*. Gabriola Island, BC, Canada: New Society Publishers, 2006.

Black, Edwin. *Internal Combustion: How Corporations and Governments Addicted the World to Oil and Derailed the Alternatives*. Santa Ana, CA: Griffin Publishing, 2008.

Evans, Robert L. *Fueling Our Future: An Introduction to Sustainable Energy*. New York, NY: Cambridge University Press, 2007.

Gilbert, Richard, and Anthony Perl. *Transport Revolutions: Moving People and Freight Without Oil*. London, England: Earthscan, 2008.

Harrington, Jonathan. *The Climate Diet: How You Can Cut Carbon, Cut Costs, and Save the Planet*. London, England: Earthscan, 2008.

Heintzmann, Andrew, and Evan Solomon, eds. *Food and Fuel: Solutions for the Future*. Toronto, ON, Canada: House of Anansi Press, 2009.

Humes, Edward. *Eco Barons: The Dreamers, Schemers, and Millionaires Who Are Saving Our Planet*. New York, NY: HarperCollins/Ecco, 2009.

Lomborg, Bjorn. *Cool It—The Skeptical Environmentalist's Guide to Global Warming*. Toronto, ON, Canada: Knopf, 2007.

Melville, Greg. *Greasy Rider: Two Dudes, One Fry-Oiled-Powered Car, and a Cross-Country Search for a Greener Future*. Chapel Hill, NC: Algonquin Books, 2008.

Morris, Neil. *Biomass Power*. North Mankato, MN: Smart Apple Media, 2007.

Orwell, George. *Animal Farm*. New York, NY: Harcourt Brace, 2003.

Povey, Karen D. *Biofuels*. Detroit, MI: KidHaven Press, 2007.

Sivertsen, Linda, and Tosh Sivertsen. *Generation Green: The Ultimate Teen Guide to Living an Eco-Friendly Life*. New York, NY: Simon Pulse, 2008.

Smith, Alisa, and J. B. MacKinnon. *Plenty: Eating Locally on the 100-Mile Diet*. New York, NY: Random House/Three Rivers Press, 2008.

Starbuck, Jon, and Gavin D. J. Harper. *Run Your Diesel Vehicle on Biofuel: A Do-It-Yourself Guide*. New York, NY: McGraw-Hill, 2009.

Twidell, John, and Anthony D. Weir. *Renewable Energy Resources*. 2nd ed. New York, NY: Taylor & Francis, 2006.

Walker, Niki. *Biomass: Fueling Change*. New York, NY: Crabtree Publishing, 2007.

Bibliography

Astyk, Sharon. "Ethics of Biofuels." *Energy Bulletin*, December 28, 2006. Retrieved April 14, 2009 (http://www.energybulletin.net/node/24169).

BBC News. "Quick Guide: Biofuels." January 24, 2007. Retrieved March 6, 2009 (http://news.bbc.co.uk/2/hi/science/nature/6294133.stm).

Berthiaume, Stephanie. "Conflict and Controversy of Alternative Fuels: The Ethics of Ethanol." *Technology*, May 23, 2008. Retrieved April 14, 2009 (http://www.associatedcontent.com/article/769521/conflict_and_controversy_of_alternative_pg2.html?cat=58).

Biello, David. "Future Solutions: Green Jet Fuels." *Scientific American*, March 2009. Retrieved April 15, 2009 (http://www.sciam.com/article.cfm?id=future-solutions-greenjet-fuels).

Bilton, Richard. "Our World: Brazil's Bitter Harvest." *BBC World News*, March 4, 2009. Retrieved March 6, 2009 (http://www.bbcworldnews.com/Pages/ProgrammeFeature.aspx?id=106&FeatureId=1057).

Dyer, Gwynne. "Feedbacks: How Much, How Fast?" *Climate Wars*. New York, NY: Random House, 2008.

Ehrenreich, Barbara. *This Land Is Their Land*. New York, NY: Henry Holt, 2008.

Evans, Robert L. *Fueling Our Future: An Introduction to Sustainable Energy*. New York, NY: Cambridge University Press, 2007.

FAO Newsroom. "UN Weighs Impact of Bioenergy: Comprehensive Report Offers Policy Framework for Decision Makers." May 8, 2007. Retrieved March 10, 2009 (http://www.fao.org/newsroom/en/news/2007/1000553/index.html).

Gingrich, Newt, and Terry L. Maple. *A Contract with the Earth*. New York, NY: Penguin Books, 2008.

Krauss, Clifford. "Valero Energy, the Oil Refiner, Wins an Auction for 7 Ethanol Plants." *New York Times*, March 19, 2009, p. B3.

Kunzig, Robert. "Our Invisible Energy." *Discover*, August 2008, p. 54

LaFraniere, Sharon. "Graft in China Covers Up Toll of Coal Mines." *New York Times*, April 10, 2009, p. A1.

Little, Jane Braxton. "The Ogallala Aquifer: Saving a Vital U.S. Water Source." *Scientific American*, March 2009, p. 39.

Mason, Jeff. "Obama to Discuss Energy, G20 Summit in Lula Meeting." *Globe and Mail*, March 14, 2009, p. B1.

McElroy, Anduin Kirkbride. "Certified: Sustainable." *Biodiesel Magazine*, June 2007, p. 27.

Melville, Greg. *Greasy Rider: Two Dudes, One Fry Oil-Powered Car, and a Cross-Country Search for a Greener Future*. Chapel Hill, NC: Algonquin Books, 2008.

Monbiot, George. "One Shot Left." *Guardian*, November 25, 2008. Retrieved January 15, 2009 (http://www. monbiot.com/archives/2008/11/25/one-shot-left).

Nash, James. "Ethanol as an Alternative Fuel Source." Content for Reprint, October 10, 2008. Retrieved April 13, 2009 (http://www.content4reprint.com/environment/ ethanol-as-an-alternative-fuel-source.htm).

Paul, Helena. "Are Biofuels Causing More Harm Than Good?" Business & Human Rights Resource Center, June 29, 2007. Retrieved February 18, 2009 (http:// www.business-humanrights.org/Links/Repository/ 699410).

Paul, Helena. "Biofuels 2.0." *The Ecologist*, February 2009, p. 14.

Pollan, Michael. "We Are What We Eat." Center for Eco-literacy, 2005. Retrieved January 25, 2009 (http://www. ecoliteracy.org/publications/rsl/michael-pollan.html).

Smith, Sara Hope. "On Target at the Sustainable Biodiesel Summit." *In Business*, March 2007. Retrieved March 20, 2009 (http://www.jgpress.com/ inbusiness/archives/_free/001297.html).

Sperling, Daniel, and Deborah Gordon. *Two Billion Cars: Driving Toward Sustainability*. New York, NY: Oxford University Press, 2009.

Zeeman, Frank. "Sucking CO_2." *Quirks and Quarks*, CBC Radio One, January 3, 2009. Retrieved February 21, 2009 (http://www.cbc.ca/quirks/archives.htm).

Index

human rights, 43
hydroelectricity, 12, 45

I

Industrial Revolution, 5, 8
internal combustion engine, 14

K

kitchen killer, 13–14

L

Lear Steam Car, 14

M

marginal land, 31, 34–35
methane, 18–20

N

nitrogen, 7
nuclear energy, 12, 45

O

Ogalla aquifer, 29–30
100-mile dinners, 51
Orwell, George, 41

P

pyrolysis, 32, 33

S

solar energy, 6–7, 45
Sustainable Biodiesel Alliance,
    20–21
sustainable development, 21–22,
    30, 47, 48
Suzuki, David, 40
synthesis gas, 33

T

This Land Is Their Land, 51
Three R's , 50

U

UN-Energy, 13, 48

W

Wiwa, Ken, 40

Y

yeast, 24, 36–37

About the Author

Paula Johanson has worked as a writer and teacher for more than twenty years, writing and editing books. Her most recent titles for Rosen Publishing are *Making Good Choices About Fair Trade* (Green Matters) and *Jobs in Sustainable Agriculture* (Green Careers). At two or more conferences each year, Johanson leads panel discussions on practical science and how it applies to home life and creative work. An accredited teacher, she has written and edited educational materials for the Alberta Distance Learning Centre and eTraffic Solutions in Canada. Instead of owning a car, Johanson is a member of a CarShare Co-operative, takes buses, and rides a delta tricycle.

Photo Credits

Cover (top left) © David Paul Morris/Getty Images; cover (top right) © Steve McAlister/Getty Images; cover (bottom) © www.istockphoto.com/ Karl Naundorf; pp. 4, 15 © Peter Dazely/Getty Images; p. 9 © Washington State Department of Ecology; pp. 13, 17, 23, 26, 28, 38, 44 © AP Photos; pp. 16, 20 © John Moore/Getty Images; p. 24 © www.istockphoto.com/ Heather Nemec; p. 31 © www.istockphoto.com/Julie Fisher; p. 32 © Jim West/Getty Images; p. 33 © Newscom; p. 35 © Robert Harding/Getty Images; pp. 40, 42 © SambaPhoto/Paolo Friedman/Getty Images.

Designer: Tom Forget; Editor: Kathy Kuhtz Campbell;
Photo Researcher: Marty Levick